Jodi Picoult
Writer

Drew Johnson & Ray Snyder with Rodney Ramos *(chapters 1 & 2)*
Terry Dodson & Rachel Dodson *(chapters 3 & 4)*
Paco Diaz *(chapter 5)*
Artists

Alex Sinclair Lee Loughridge Dave McCaig
Colorists

Rob Leigh Travis Lanham
Letterers

Terry Dodson & Rachel Dodson with Alex Sinclair
Original covers

DER WOMAN

Love and Murder

Wonder Woman created by William Moulton Marston

Dan DiDio
Senior VP-Executive Editor

Matt Idelson
Editor-original series

Nachie Castro
Associate Editor-original series

Anton Kawasaki
Editor-collected edition

Robbin Brosterman
Senior Art Director

Paul Levitz
President & Publisher

Georg Brewer
VP-Design & DC Direct Creative

Richard Bruning
Senior VP-Creative Director

Patrick Caldon
Executive VP-Finance & Operations

Chris Caramalis
VP-Finance

John Cunningham
VP-Marketing

Terri Cunningham
VP-Managing Editor

Alison Gill
VP-Manufacturing

Hank Kanalz
VP-General Manager, WildStorm

Jim Lee
Editorial Director-WildStorm

Paula Lowitt
Senior VP-Business & Legal Affairs

MaryEllen McLaughlin
VP-Advertising & Custom Publishing

John Nee
VP-Business Development

Gregory Noveck
Senior VP-Creative Affairs

Sue Pohja
VP-Book Trade Sales

Cheryl Rubin
Senior VP-Brand Management

Jeff Trojan
VP-Business Development, DC Direct

Bob Wayne
VP-Sales

Cover by Terry Dodson &
Rachel Dodson with Alex Sinclair

WONDER WOMAN:
LOVE AND MURDER

JODI PICOULT

i n t r o d u c t i o n

When DC Comics first approached me to write the Wonder Woman comic book series, my immediate thought was that I didn't have time to devote to it, given the fact that I was supposed to be writing a novel. My second thought was that it was far too cool an opportunity to pass up (something my children immediately reiterated). I decided to undertake the challenge for a few reasons — because it was something I'd never done before; because I'd always been a fan of Wonder Woman (who hasn't?); because I'd admired other writers who'd seamlessly moved between fiction and comic books (Brad Meltzer foremost); and because I would be only the second woman to write the comic book in its long history.

I have never had so much fun writing — nor worked so hard. The chance to flex my comedic muscles, the balance of fitting a story into twenty-two pages, and the task of keeping Wonder Woman's long history as a character intact all weighed heavily upon me. Most daunting of all: how could I put my fingerprint on Wonder Woman? Why, of all the writers in the world, had DC Comics asked ME to take her on?

My first attempt to effect subtle change was to take her out of her bustier, as any woman writer would know it's impossible to fight crime without straps. I was soundly rejected. But when I seriously began to think of Wonder Woman and my own impressions of her, I knew what I'd have to do: create a storyline that captured her wide demographic of fans — from young women looking for a role model to adults who'd grown up with her, male and female — and create a richness and depth of character that had previously been missing. Like Superman, Wonder Woman's larger than life. But unlike Clark Kent, Wonder Woman's "human" identities have been underdeveloped. It was easy for readers to admire her, and hard for them to relate to her. To that end, I began to think about today's term, "wonder women," which is used to refer to women who do it all...and usually feel like they're not doing any of it well enough! What if Wonder Woman continued to be the strongest, smartest female on this planet...but had some doubt in other areas of her life? Not in a way that weakened her...but that made her, well, more human? What if she were worried, like the rest of us, about not fitting in with the people we like the most? What if she struggled with being who she wanted and needed to be...and not just who her parents intended? These are universal battles, and it seemed to me that Wonder Woman was plenty strong enough to undertake them.

I chose to bring back Circe because she was my favorite villain — a smart, savvy woman, whose motivation for wreaking havoc is not as simple as it seems, but is actually also related to the people she loves the most. And I also chose to bring back Wonder Woman's mother, Hippolyta, because I wanted Wonder Woman to have a psychological foil just as strong as she is. Even those of us who command complete control, after all, usually bow to our parents' wishes. But what if our parents' wishes strike at the core of who we are?

The cliffhanger in LOVE AND MURDER was important to me. Not only was it a fantastic ending that would leave people gasping — it also was a wonderful starting point for the next writer who'd inherit the series after me. But most of all, it illustrated what I wanted in my arc: a Wonder Woman who reflects upon her previous actions and realizes that what we convince ourselves is right might now, in hindsight, be as innocent as we believed at the time; a Wonder Woman who is strong enough psychologically as well as physically to stand up to her mother and say that there's a difference between love and duty — and who is willing to put her own life at stake to teach her mother that lesson as well.

This series has been one of the high points of my writing career; I hope you enjoy it as well.

Jodi Picoult
June 2007

Maxwell Lord, the "Black King" of the government agency known as Checkmate, had been secretly gathering sensitive information on the world's super-heroes. Using his mental powers, Lord was able to take control of the mind of the world's most powerful hero, Superman, and used the Man of Steel to beat up Batman and attack Wonder Woman. The Amazing Amazon eventually bound Lord in her "lasso of truth," forcing Lord to tell her how to stop the rampaging Superman from potentially causing countless deaths and massive destruction. Lord replied with the only solution available: "Kill me."

Seeing no other choice, Wonder Woman snapped Lord's neck, freeing Superman. But both the Man of Steel and the Dark Knight could not condone Wonder Woman's actions — believing that there could have been another way to stop Lord. Following this tragic event, Wonder Woman took a year off from her duties to do some soul-searching, and also adopted the identity of Diana Prince — a special agent for the Department of Metahuman Affairs. Diana is partnered with Nemesis, a master of disguise, and the two report to Sarge Steel. She now divides her time between her government job and her original mission of bringing peace to "Man's World" as Wonder-Woman.

But that peace is about to be shattered...

I CAN'T BELIEVE I MISSED WONDER WOMAN!...I BET SHE LOOKED HOT.

WHAT ARE YOU, TWELVE?

THANKS FOR SHOPPING AT THE HERO S

BE A HERO! BUY HERO STUFF!

I THOUGHT SARGE WANTED US BACK AT HEADQUARTERS.

RELAX, I JUST NEED TO GET MY NIECE A BIRTHDAY GIFT.

THE BATMAN ONE'S BETTER. LOOK--IT'S GOT A DETACHABLE BATARANG... BUT MY--ER, WONDER WOMAN'S LASSO DOESN'T EVEN COME OFF.

TRUST ME, MY NIECE'LL LOVE IT...

I THOUGHT YOU WERE AN ONLY CHILD...?

BE A HER BUY HERO STUFF!

ALL WONDER WOMAN STUFF IS 75% OFF.

SWEET!

UM... WHY?

WONDER WOMAN'S NOT COOL, I GUESS.

DOESN'T SAVING THE WORLD ALL THE TIME MAKE YOU COOL?

ALL I KNOW IS SHE'S NEVER SOLD AS WELL AS SUPERMAN OR BATMAN...

75% OFF! SWEET!

HUMANS ARE ALL ABOUT FILLING EVERYTHING. YOU WORK HARD TO FILL YOUR WALLET TO BUY STUFF TO FILL YOUR HOUSE...

WE'RE OUT OF GAS. I'LL PUMP-- YOU PAY.

...OR IN MY CASE, A *VERY SMALL* APARTMENT.

UH, GAS IS $3 A GALLON, SWEETHEART. THAT MIGHT GET US DOWN THE BLOCK...

YOU NEED A CAR TO GET TO WORK TO FILL YOUR WALLET, AND THEN YOU NEED TO FILL YOUR CAR...

YOU HAVE A CREDIT CARD, RIGHT?

CREDIT CARD?

IF YOU WORK HARD, YOU CAN AFFORD TO GET A BIGGER CAR TO TAKE YOU TO WORK...

GEEZ, HOW DO YOU NORMALLY GET AROUND? *FLY* OR SOMETHING?

HA, HA. FUNNY. FLY PLACES. IMAGINE...!

AND YOU CAN WORK MORE TO AFFORD TO GET A BIGGER HOUSE TO FILL WITH MORE STUFF.

TEN BUCKS? NO CREDIT CARD? WHERE ARE YOU FROM? MARS? NEW HAMPSHIRE?

I THOUGHT BEING HUMAN WOULD BE EASY...

FORGET IT. I'LL PAY. YOU PUMP.

I MAY HAVE BEEN WRONG.

PUMP?

MY JOB IS TO BRING IN WONDER WOMAN...

BUT HOW CAN I, WITHOUT REVEALING WHO I TRULY AM?

WONDER WOMAN... WOW. I *CAN'T* BELIEVE THIS IS MY JOB.

EVERY QUESTION I ASK IS ANSWERED WITH MORE QUESTIONS...

WHAT DO YOU THINK THE GOVERNMENT WANTS TO ASK HER?

THE GUY SHE KILLED WAS A GOVERNMENT AGENT. A CORRUPT ONE... BUT STILL. THE GOVERNMENT TAKES CARE OF ITS OWN... AND WONDER WOMAN'S NOT ONE OF ITS OWN.

ICED DOUBLE VENTE SOY LATTE, WITH TURBINADO SUGAR, PLEASE.

UM... SMALL CUP OF COFFEE?

VENTI, DUOVENT, GRANDE, OR UBER?

I DON'T THI[N]K SHE SPEAK[S] ENGLISH...

UM... SMALL CUP OF COFFEE.

I ALREADY KNOW EVERYTHING THERE IS TO KNOW ABOUT THESE BRACELETS.

THEY'RE COPIES OF MY REAL ONES.

THEY WERE DESIGNED TO COMPLETE A UNIFORM I DONATED TO THE WONDER WOMAN MUSEUM...

...WHICH CLOSED DOWN OVER A YEAR AGO.

BUT AT LEAST NOW I KNOW WHERE TO START LOOKING FOR TOM...

...AND WHOEVER'S PRETENDING TO BE ME.

ONCE, AS PRINCESS DIANA OF THE AMAZONS, ALL THESE ARTIFACTS WERE MINE...

NOW, IT IS LOST.

NOW I'M DIANA PRINCE, SPECIAL AGENT FOR THE DEPARTMENT OF METAHUMAN AFFAIRS.

AS AGENT PRINCE, I LOST MY PARTNER, TOM TRESSER, A.K.A. NEMESIS.

HE WAS KIDNAPPED, AND LEFT BEHIND WERE AN OLD PAIR OF MY BRACELETS.

BRACELETS THAT I KNEW BELONGED HERE...

...IF ONLY
I KNEW WHERE
I BELONG.

HE'S LOSING A LOT OF BLOOD...

WHERE'RE WE GOING?

...BUT, SINCE I AM A "FUGITIVE" ONCE MORE...

...A HOSPITAL IS TOO RISKY.

YOU KNOW, I'M NOT USED TO GETTING RESCUED BY GIRLS...

CIRCE MADE IT SEEM AS IF I'M REMOVED FROM HUMANITY...

DONATE YOUR OLD CAR TO FIGHT HOMELESSNESS.

5TH ST. VETERINARIAN CLINIC

3725

MINI

...BUT I DON'T ENJOY BEING FORCED TO BREAK THEIR RULES.

YOU'RE USED TO GETTING RESCUED BY WHAT, THEN? BOYS?

WHAT I'M DOING NOW IS WRONG-- I KNOW THAT...

...BUT YOU CAN DO SOMETHING WRONG AND TELL YOURSELF IT'S RIGHT.

KRRSSH

SHERYL J. VETERINARY LARGE &

BEEP BEEP BEE

I'VE DONE IT BEFORE...

THAT'S NOT WHAT I MEANT, AND YOU KNOW IT...

...AND MAYBE THAT'S WHAT SCARES ME THE MOST.

I'M NO DOCTOR, BUT NEMESIS SHOULD BE BACK TO NORMAL...

THANKS--NO ONE'S EVER TAKEN ME TO THE VET BEFORE.

AS NORMAL AS HE GETS, ANYWAY...

I HAVEN'T EATEN SINCE I WAS KIDNAPPED... YOU THINK THESE ARE SAFE?

RABIES SHOT...?

UM...NO THANKS.

I WAS KIDDING.

I WISH I COULD WORK WITH YOU.

MY PARTNER, ON THE OTHER HAND... MAN, WHAT A TOOL.

WORK WITH ME? AREN'T YOU SUPPOSED TO BE ARRESTING ME?

I DON'T ALWAYS DO WHAT I'M TOLD. ESPECIALLY WHEN I GET THE FEELING I'M NOT BEING TOLD EVERYTHING.

BY THE GODS!

QUEEN MOTHER, YOU'RE ALIVE!

IT'S A BLESSING...

BUT HOW?

WHY WOULD YOU DO THIS FOR US?

BECAUSE THE ENEMY OF MY ENEMY IS MY FRIEND.

MY QUEEN, YOU NEED TO SEE THIS.

MY DAUGHTER!

IS IN GRAVE DANGER. YOU *ALL* ARE.

IT IS ALWAYS THE SAME WITH THE WORLD OF MAN. WHAT THEY DON'T UNDERSTAND, THEY FEAR.

AND WHAT THEY FEAR, THEY TRY TO TAME.

TO THEM, MY DAUGHTER IS THE ENEMY...

AND ENEMIES MUST BE CRUSHED.

IF IT IS WA[R] THAT TH[EY] WANT.

"'S WAR THAT 'EY'LL GET."

VILLAINS & VIXENS BAR. WASHINGTON, DC.

DAMMIT, DIANA! ANSWER THE PHONE!

GIRLFRIEND WON'T TAKE YOUR CALLS, TOMMY?

IT'S MY PARTNER. SHE PROBABLY CAN'T FIGURE OUT *HOW*.

WOMEN. CAN'T LIVE WITH THEM, CAN'T LIVE WITHOUT THEM.

LULU, YOU, UM...*ARE* THEM.

AND YOU THOUGHT IT WAS COMPLICATED FOR *YOU*.

BZZZZZ

TRESSER. OKAY, I'LL BE RIGHT THERE.

OKAY, MR. ICICLE GUY. UP, UP AND AWAY.

FAR AWAY, PREFERABLY...

WAS THAT YOUR PARTNER CHICK?

NO, THE BOSS. GOTTA RUN.

THA'S JUS' THE PROBLEM WITH FLASH. HE'S SO...LIKE... FAST!!!

THANKS FOR THE BEER AND THE COMPANY, LULU.

ANYTIME, TOMMY. DRIVE SAFE. OR FLY SAFE. OR WHATEVER.

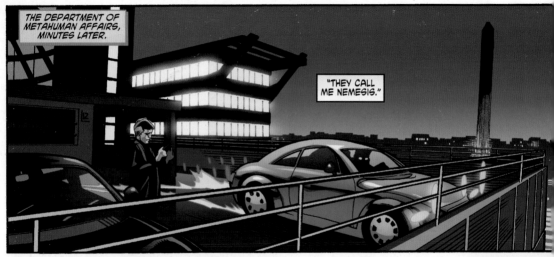

THE DEPARTMENT OF METAHUMAN AFFAIRS, MINUTES LATER.

"THEY CALL ME NEMESIS."

TOM, THE REASON YOU'VE BEEN UNABLE TO CONTACT AGENT PRINCE IS BECAUSE SHE'S BEEN REASSIGNED.

BUT--THE WONDER WOMAN ASSIGNMENT--

IS CLOSED, TOM.

"AS I'VE RECENTLY BEEN REMINDED, MY NAME MEANS 'ENEMY'..."

YOU KNOW THIS IS A FRAME-UP, SARGE. IF I COULD JUST TALK TO WONDER WOMAN--

THE DEFENSE DEPARTMENT TOOK HER INTO CUSTODY...

"'CUSTODY' BEING A TERM THE POWERS-THAT-BE ARE NOW USING ON ANYONE WHO STANDS IN THE WAY OF THEIR OWN LUST FOR CONTROL."

...AND I DON'T HAVE A CLUE WHERE THEY'VE TAKEN HER.

THEN FIND OUT!

WHY IS SHE SUDDENLY THE ENEMY? HOW IS CIRCE INVOLVED?

DOESN'T EVERYTHING ABOUT THIS SEEM WRONG TO YOU?

"BUT IN NAMING WONDER WOMAN THE 'ENEMY,' THEY'VE CROSSED THE LINE."

TOM, *YOU'RE* BEING REASSIGNED, TOO.

LET ME FREAKIN' GUESS. TOP PRIORITY. URGENT.

I HAVE TO BE IN PORTLAND FREAKIN' OREGON BY TOMORROW.

"TO ME, WONDER WOMAN'S SYNONYMOUS WITH EVERYTHING GOOD ABOUT THIS CRUDDY WORLD. SHE SAVED ME, AND I'M JUST ONE OF MANY."

PORTLAND, MAINE, ACTUALLY.

BUT AN AMAZING GUESS.

IT'S NO GUESS, SARGE. I FEEL SOMETHING YANKING ON MY PUPPET STRINGS, THAT'S ALL.

PUPPET STRINGS? *HA--* WHAT DOES *THAT* FEEL LIKE?

HARD TO SAY... LIKE AN ANGEL HAVING ITS WINGS TORN OFF.

"AND AS FOR MY OWN NAME...

"...I'M ABOUT TO LIVE UP TO IT."

YOU'RE NO ANGEL, TOM.

PEOPLE CHANGE.

WHO'S REALLY THE HERO HERE, AND WHO'S THE VILLAIN? THE GIRL WHO FIGHTS FOR GOOD BECAUSE IT'S HER DUTY...

OR THE GIRL WHO FIGHTS FOR WHAT SHE LOVES, NO MATTER WHAT IT TAKES TO GET IT?

YOU'RE TAKING RIGHT AND WRONG OUT OF THE EQUATION.

YOU TALK ABOUT THEM LIKE THEY'RE SET IN STONE.

THEY ARE! THAT'S WHY I FIGHT FOR ONE AGAINST THE OTHER.

REALLY? WASN'T IT ONCE "RIGHT" TO OWN SLAVES IN THIS ADOPTED COUNTRY OF YOURS? TO BEAT YOUR WIFE?

TO FORCE SOMEONE ELSE TO BELIEVE IN YOUR GOD? TO KILL THEM IF THEY DIDN'T?

DON'T YOU GET IT? WHAT'S CONSIDERED RIGHT TODAY COULD BE WRONG TOMORROW.

AND WHAT LOOKS WRONG NOW... MIGHT TURN OUT TO BE RIGHT ALL ALONG.

WHAT MAKES YOU THINK I'D BELIEVE ANYTHING YOU HAVE TO SAY TO ME? WHY ARE YOU EVEN HERE? WHY?

BECAUSE LOVE AND MURDER ARE THE ONLY THINGS THAT MATTER.

THEY'RE WHAT IT MEANS TO BE HUMAN.

AND IF THAT'S THE CASE, I WILL ALWAYS BE MORE HUMAN THAN YOU.

TELL THAT TO MAXWELL LORD, DARLING. THEN TRY TELLING IT...

...TO YOURSELF.

MURDER DOESN'T MAKE YOU HUMAN.

WELL, WELL-- WHAT DO WE HAVE HERE?

CLICK

RRRUMMBBBLE

WHOA...

WHA-- SOMEONE GOT IN THERE! HOW?

SECURITY, THIS IS AGENT VANLEER-- SOUND THE ALARM.

I REPEAT-- IS ANYONE THERE?

LOOK ON THE BRIGHT SIDE--AT LEAST SHE'S STOPPED TALKING TO HERSELF...

RRRUMMBBBLE

SARGE? WHERE DID YOU--er...

NO ONE'S ALLOWED ACCESS HERE, SIR, NOT EVEN YOU. I'M SORRY, BUT YOU SAID SO YOURSELF, SIR.

THAT'S PRETTY DUMB, GENTLEMEN. IF I HAVE THE AUTHORITY TO ORDER YOU TO DENY ME ACCESS, I ALSO HAVE THE AUTHORITY TO DENY MY PREVIOUS ORDER TO DENY ME ACCESS.

Um...COULD YOU REPEAT THAT, SIR?

WELL, DO YOU REALLY THINK I WOULD ISSUE SUCH AN IDIOTIC ORDER?

WELL, NO, SIR--BUT YOU TOLD US IN PERSON--

THWONK

STEEL? WHAT DO YOU WANT FROM ME NOW?

CLICK

AAROUUGH

THE ALARMS! CRAP!

YOU'D BETTER BE PREPARED TO KILL ME, BECAUSE I WON'T TELL YOU ANYTHING WHILE THERE'S STILL BREATH LEFT IN MY BODY!

I'D BACK OFF IF I WERE YOU...

GO TO HELL!

NO, I MEAN IT. BACK OFF, WONDER WOMAN.

LIKE, LITERALLY.

...BLISTERS... CHICKEN POX...

GOSH, ALL I'VE GOT IS THIS SPACE-AGE EPOXY...BUT I WOULDN'T USE IT IF I WERE YOU.

I'M PRETTY SURE IF IT COMES IN CONTACT WITH BARE SKIN IT CAUSES BOILS...

JUST GIVE ME THE DAMN GLUE.

YOUR EYES ARE CLOSED, RIGHT?

Uh...RIGHT. CLEARLY YOU AMAZONS HAVE A LOT TO BE INSECURE ABOUT AESTHETICALLY.

IT'S NOT A MATTER OF *INSECURITY*--

--IT'S A MATTER OF... DECENCY.

I'LL TELL YOU WHAT'S DECENT. THAT BIRTHMARK ON YOUR--

YOU'RE A *PIG*, YOU KNOW THAT?!

WELL, *YOU*, COINCIDENTALLY, ARE A PAIN IN THE SAME PLACE YOU'VE GOT THAT BIRTHMARK!

IF THE AMAZONS WERE AIMING FOR THE WHITE HOUSE, THEY FAILED.

IF THEY WERE AIMING FOR A METAPHOR, THEY SUCCEEDED.

I NEVER KNOW IF YOU'RE KIDDING OR NOT.

WONDER WOMAN!

I WAS BEGINNING TO WONDER IF YOU'D SHOW UP. SUPERMAN SAYS YOUR MOTHER IS LEADING THE AMAZON FIGHT.

WHICH, BY THE WAY, IS IMPOSSIBLE. I SAW HER DIE.

IT'S NOT REALLY HIPPOLYTA. SHE'S A FAKE, OR A DOPPELGANGER OR SOMETHING.

HEY!

THEN SOMEONE WHO LOOKS LIKE YOUR DEAD MOTHER JUST DESTROYED THE WASHINGTON MONUMENT.

THIS IS BAD.

YOU KNOW FOR A FACT THIS ISN'T YOUR MOTHER?

I'M GOING TO...

YOU'LL NEED TO ACT QUICKLY. THIS BATTLE IS LAYING WASTE TO THE CITY.

SO FAR WE'VE BEEN ABLE TO CONTAIN THE FIGHT WITHIN THE DISTRICT AND AVOID MASS CASUALTIES... BUT WE WON'T BE ABLE TO DO THAT MUCH LONGER.

I DON'T UNDERSTAND *WHY* MY PEOPLE WOULD ATTACK.

WE ASSUMED IT HAD SOMETHING TO DO WITH YOU.

WELL, I *WAS* WRONGLY IMPRISONED BY THE DEPARTMENT OF METAHUMAN AFFAIRS.

WHY DON'T YOU WATCH WHERE YOU LAND?

WHAT?

WELL, YOU'RE PROBABLY SOFTER THAN SUPERMAN, SWEETHEART.

SARGE STEEL SAID IT HAD TO DO WITH MAX LORD...BUT HE WAS ASKING A *LOT* OF QUESTIONS ABOUT THE AMAZONIAN PURPLE DEATH RAY.

THAT... DOESN'T MAKE ANY SENSE.

NONE OF THIS DOES. WHY WOULD THE AMAZONS SUDDENLY ATTACK THE UNITED STATES, PARTICULARLY GIVEN THE SUPERHERO POPULATION HERE? IT'S A BATTLE THEY CAN'T WIN...

CALL ME SWEETHEART AGAIN AND I'LL KICK YOUR BUTT SO HARD YOU'LL BE GAGGING ON MY BOOT UNTIL CHRISTMAS.

WILL YOU QUIT FOCUSING ON MY BUTT?

I KNOW IT'S SEXY, BUT WE'VE ONLY JUST MET.

THE FIRST THING TO DO IS CONFRONT MY "MOTHER" AND GET TO THE BOTTOM OF THIS.

I'LL NEED TO TAKE NEMESIS ALONG FOR, *uh...* BACKUP.

HEY!

I THOUGHT YOU WORKED *ALONE!*

WHEN YOU LOSE SOMEONE YOU LOVE, YOU SPEND THE REST OF YOUR LIFE WISHING YOU HAD JUST ONE MORE MOMENT WITH THEM.

I LOOK AT THIS WOMAN WITH THE FACE OF MY MOTHER, AND EVEN THOUGH I KNOW IT CAN'T BE TRUE...

DIANA!

MOTHER...?

...SOMETHING IN ME HOPES I'VE ACTUALLY BEEN GIVEN THAT CHANCE.

IN MY MIND, I DON'T WANT THIS WOMAN-- WHO'S STARTED A WAR, AND CAUSED ALL THIS DESTRUCTION-- TO BE MY MOTHER...

I THOUGHT I'D NEVER SEE YOU AGAIN...

YOU'RE... YOU WERE DEAD. HOW...?

DID THEY HURT YOU?

BUT IN MY HEART, THERE'S NOTHING I WANT MORE.

MOTHER-- YOU'VE MISUNDERSTOOD. I'M FREE. THE GOVERNMENT--

TOOK YOU PRISONER!

HOW COULD SI KNOW THAT? T ONLY PEOPLE WHO KNEW ABC MY IMPRISONME WERE NEMES AND...CIRCE.

YOU'RE ATTACKING INNOCENT PEOPLE!

DO NOT DEFEND THEIR CRIMES! YOU SHOULD BE FIGHTING BESIDE US!

WORDS CAN'T CONVEY THE *TROUBLE* YOU'RE IN, AGENT TRESSER.

C'MON, SARGE. THINK OF OLD TIMES-- DRINKING TEQUILA AT VILLAINS AND VIXENS WITH ROCCO, THE BARTENDER...

"SARGE HAS LIED TO ME AT LEAST TWICE, RECENTLY..."

"...I'VE STARTED TO THINK HE MAY NOT REALLY *BE* SARGE."

ROCCO AND I CAN DRINK TEQUILA FOR YOU--

--WHILE YOU'RE SERVING TIME FOR BREAKING A PRISONER OUT OF A FEDERAL FACILITY.

THAT'S FINE-- EXCEPT THE BARTENDER'S NAME IS LULU, THE SARGE I KNOW HATES TEQUILA, AND *YOU'RE* CLEARLY A *LYING*--

TOM! LOOK OUT!

SARGE?

I HOPE TOM KNOWS WHAT HE'S DOING...

DIANA! SO GOOD TO SEE YOU IN THE FREE WORLD AGAIN!

DID YOU POST BAIL?

CIRCE!!!

WHAT DID YOU DO TO MY MOTHER?!?

I BROUGHT HER BACK FROM THE DEAD FOR YOU, DARLING.

YOU'RE WELCOME.

THAT'S NOT MY MOTHER. SHE'S A FAKE. OR YOU'VE POSSESSED HER----SO THAT SHE'D ATTACK THE VERY PEOPLE SHE ONCE SENT ME TO DEFEND!

POSSESSED HER? THE QUEEN IS QUITE REAL AND CONTROLS HER OWN ACTIONS, I ASSURE YOU.

BUT MY MOTHER WOULD NEVER--

BEING DEAD MAKES YOU WEIRD, DARLING. JUST LOOK AT THE SPICE GIRLS.

OR CHICAGO CUBS FANS.

DEPARTMENT OF METAHUMAN AFFAIRS.

INTERROGATION ROOM #7.

THIS IS *ABSURD!* HOW IS KNOWING MY SOCIAL SECURITY NUMBER GOING TO TELL YOU *I'M* ME AND *HE'S* AN IMPOSTOR?

062-54-7919. AND MY FAVORITE ACTRESS IS NATALIE PORTMAN, AND I HATE TEQUILA.

OKAY, WHAT'S YOUR MOTHER'S MAIDEN NAME, SARGE... *uh*...NUMBER ONE?

THIS IS AN OUTRAGE! LOCK HIM UP!

YOU REALLY WANT TO KNOW WHO THE *FAKE* SARGE IS? HAND ME A PEN...

"HOPE I KNOW WHAT I'M DOING..."

A HANDWRITING TEST-- EXCELLENT IDEA.

THREE IDEAS, ACTUALLY. FIRST, ANYONE WHO KNOWS ME KNOWS I LOST MY *HAND*--AND WEAR A *METAL* PROSTHESIS.

SHINFÉEE!!!

SECOND, *METAL* DOESN'T BLEED.

AND LAST OF ALL...

...YOU'RE ALL *FIRED.*

"WHEN YOU BOIL IT DOWN, WAR IS JUST A CHESS GAME.

"YOU DON'T MAKE A SINGLE MOVE WITHOUT A REASON.

"THING IS, IT MAY TAKE A WHOLE GAME BEFORE THAT REASON IS APPARENT.

"FIRST MOVE: GIVE THE GOVERNMENT REASON TO FEAR THE AMAZON'S POWER.

"SECOND MOVE: GIVE THE AMAZONS REASON TO FEAR THE GOVERNMENT'S POWER.

"THIRD MOVE: GET RID OF SARGE, AND PUT A MOLE IN HIS PLACE...

"...WHO SEIZES WONDER WOMAN AND SETS THE PLAN IN MOTION.

"WHAT'S LEFT UNPROTECTED?

"A QUEEN WHO'S BEEN LED TO THINK SHE'S IN CONTROL.

"BUT AS ANY CHESS PLAYER KNOWS...

"...THERE'S *ALWAYS* A MORE POWERFUL PIECE ON THE BOARD.

"AND *THAT'S* WHAT YOU HAVE TO CAPTURE TO WIN."

GAME, SET AND MATCH.

WEAPON: *NUCLEAR WARHEAD*
STATUS: *ARMED, PRE-LAUNCH COUNTDOWN INITIATED*
TARGET: *774 MARK 359, THEMYSCIRA*

TIME: T-2:34:57

MOMMIE DEAREST IS AS SHE'S ALWAYS BEEN--RULED BY HER DUTY TO HER AMAZON SISTERS. *YOU* USED TO BE RULED BY DUTY, TOO.

BUT YOU'RE NO LONGER LIKE YOUR MOTHER, DARLING...YOUR FEELINGS HAVE DRIVEN YOU *HERE*--

--TO THE HUMANS, TO DESPERATION, AND-- AS OUR FRIEND MAXWELL LORD WOULD ATTEST-- TO *MURDER*.

INSTEAD OF ASKING IF THIS IS REALLY YOUR MOTHER... MAYBE YOU SHOULD BE ASKING... *WHO ARE YOU?*

DAMN YOU, CIRCE. *YOU* STARTED THIS WAR!

WELL, OF COURSE I DID! *SOMEONE* HAD TO GET THE BALL ROLLING.

BUT THE HUMANS AND THE AMAZONS WEREN'T EXACTLY ANGELS TO BEGIN WITH.

EVERYTHING'S GONE ACCORDING TO SCHEDULE, EXCEPT FOR ONE THING...

YOU. I PLANNED FOR *YOU* TO DIE, AS WELL. BUT NOW I SEE HOW WE...RELATE.

RECENT EVENTS HAVE RICOCHETED US FROM OPPOSITE ENDS OF THE SPECTRUM TO OUR CURRENT... COLLISION COURSE. WE'RE PRACTICALLY SISTERS, DARLING.

YOU'RE INSANE.

I'M THINKING THAT WHEN THIS WHOLE THING IS OVER, WE CAN GO INTO CRIME FIGHTING TOGETHER.

TRAVEL THE GLOBE, SAVING WOMEN FROM OPPRESSION...WHAT A TEAM WE'D BE!

CAN BE THE FUNNY, SASSY, SEXY ONE...

...AND YOU CAN BE THE [D]ORKY SQUARE ONE [W]HO SAYS DORKY [SQ]UARE THINGS LIKE "*GREAT HERA!*"

THOOM

I RARELY SAY THAT ANYMORE...

SHRAAAAAACK

"I CAN'T SHAKE ALL THE QUESTIONS RUNNING THROUGH MY HEAD.

"LIKE, WHY IS A NUCLEAR WEAPON AIMED TOWARD THE MIDDLE OF THE SKY?

"WHY WOULD EVERYMAN WANT TO KILL ALL THE AMAZONS?

"AND WHY DID THE COMPUTER SAY THE TARGET WAS THEMYSCIRA... IF IT'S NOT IN THIS DIMENSION, LET ALONE ON EARTH?

"AND MOST OF ALL...

"...WHO THE HELL IS HE *WORKING* FOR?"

SKREEEEEEEEEECH

ONCE UPON A TIME, I THOUGHT I WAS A HERO.

THEY CALLED ME WONDER WOMAN...

AS IF I WERE A WONDER OF THE WORLD.

THAT CONTEXT HAS CHANGED WITH DECISIONS I'VE MADE.

NOW, I JUST WONDER WHO I AM.

LIFE IS STRANGE THAT WAY...

EVERY SO OFTEN YOU AWAKEN FROM THE ACT OF SIMPLY LIVING IT...

WITH NEW QUESTIONS SCREAMING THROUGH YOUR HEAD...

QUESTIONS LIKE: "WHO AM I?"

IT'S FUNNY, THE THINGS THAT GO THROUGH YOUR HEAD...

...WHEN YOUR MOTHER IS TRYING TO KILL YOU.

YOU START TO NOTICE THE LITTLE THINGS...

NOT JUST ABOUT YOUR MOTHER AND YOURSELF...

BUT LIKE THAT BILLBOARD ACROSS THE WAY...

!VE Life!

"LIVE LIFE"? WHAT A STUPID SLOGAN.

I MEAN, DOESN'T EVERYONE DO THAT, ANYWAY?

THEN IT HITS ME-- MAYBE WHAT I'VE BEEN DOING ALL ALONG ISN'T LIVING LIFE...

MAYBE I'VE JUST BEEN AVOIDING DEATH.

AND MAYBE THERE'S A DIFFERENCE.

I'VE ALWAYS DONE WHAT'S RIGHT, BECAUSE IT'S WHAT MY MOTHER TAUGHT ME.

DOES THAT MAKE ME A HERO... OR A ROBOT?

THE HUMANS WILL LOSE THIS WAR--WHETHER YOU FIGHT WITH US OR *AGAINST* US.

YOU STARTED THIS WAR--IT CAN END ONLY WHEN I *SIEZE* THE THRONE FROM YOU!

DON'T SPEAK SO TO ME!

CRA*AACK*

Uh, WONDER WOMAN...?

HELP!!!!!

TOM!

MOTHER! WE NEED TO SAVE OUR HOME! THEMYSCIRA IS IN DANGER!

NO MORE *LIES!* PREPARE THE WEAPON!

BUT, MY QUEEN...

NOW, MARTA!

WE HAVE TO GET THAT WEAPON AWAY FROM THEM.

KNOWING CIRCE, IT'S EITHER MEANT TO KILL HUMANS, AMAZONS, OR ALL OF THE ABOVE.

WELL, HOW'S YOUR PITCHING ARM, ACE? GOOD ENOUGH TO GET ME AND YOUR MOTHER OUT OF THE COLLECTIVE VIEW?

WHAT? OH.

MY QUEEN, PERHAPS WE SHOULD RECONSIDER USING THE WEAPON. CIRCE HAS PROVEN UNTRUSTWORTHY...

HEY, HAVE I EVER STEERED YOU WRONG BEFORE?

QUEEN HIPPOLYTA...?

NO! WAIT!

STOP THAT IMPOSTOR!

THE JIG'S UP!

WHAT? NO!

TOM--DON'T OPEN IT! WE DON'T KNOW WHAT'S INSIDE!

THE IDIOT! HE'LL KILL US ALL!

UnGh!

TOM, GET RID OF IT!

IN A MINUTE...

...WHICH I, um, DON'T HAVE...

BYMMMM GMMMZ

WONDER WOMAN
Amazons Attack

WILL PFEIFER ~ PETE WOODS

KINGDOM COME

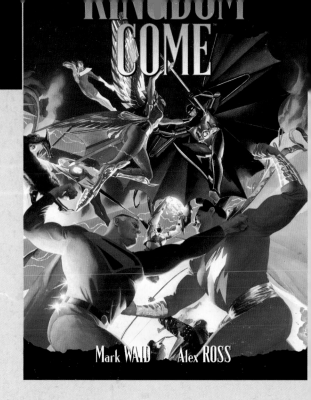

Mark Waid and Alex Ross deliver a grim tale of youth versus experience, tradition versus change and what defines a hero. KINGDOM COME is a riveting story pitting the old guard — Superman, Batman, Wonder Woman and their peers — against a new, uncompromising generation.

WINNER OF FIVE EISNER AND HARVEY AWARDS, INCLUDING BEST LIMITED SERIES AND BEST ARTIST

IDENTITY CRISIS

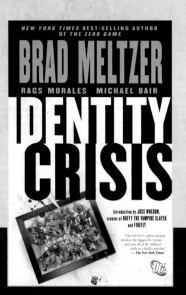

BRAD MELTZER
RAGS MORALES
MICHAEL BAIR

CRISIS ON INFINITE EARTHS

MARV WOLFMAN
GEORGE PÉREZ

DC: THE NEW FRONTIER VOLUME 1

DARWYN COOKE
DAVE STEWART